Doing *Mitzvot:*

Mitzvah Projects for Bar/Bat Mitzvah

by
Rabbi Ronald H. Isaacs
and
Rabbi Kerry M. Olitzky

Illustrated by
Rabbi Jeffrey Sirkman

KTAV Publishing House, Inc.
Hoboken, New Jersey

Manufactured in the United States of America

At thirteen, one is ready for *mitzvot*.
Pirke Avot 5:23

In honor of the Bar Mitzvah of
Avi Samuel Olitzky
Parashat Noach
3 Heshvan 5755

and the B'nai/B'not Mitzvah Students of
Temple Sholom
Bridgewater, New Jersey
and
Congregation B'nai Tikvah
North Brunswick, New Jersey

Table of Contents

A Note to Parents and Teachers

This book is designed to help your child/your student grow into Jewish adulthood the year he or she celebrates Bar/Bat Mitzvah. Unlike other project-oriented collections of this kind, this book is unique in that it is intended to introduce the Bar/Bat Mitzvah student to the world of mitzvot through the actual practice of mitzvot. It is not a simply a collection of social action projects. Rather, the book contains an articulated approach to the world of mitzvot. We believe that the practice of mitzvot contains the potential of bringing the individual closer to God. We want to help your child unleash that potential and bring the holy into his or her world. Thus, many of the mitzvot are taken from a selection of text in the Mishnah (Peah 1:1).

In these pages we offer opportunities for mitzvot every month during the Bar/Bat Mitzvah year. That's why there are twelve chapters devoted to mitzvah projects. Hopefully, these projects will be cumulative. Thus, the child can add projects each month without necessarily forgoing what took place the month before. That's also why we have stayed away from task-oriented projects that require a specific and limited investment of energy—and thus are easily forgotten once concluded. Because we believe in "doing mitzvot," the emphasis is on activity outside of the classroom rather than on the "talking heads" that take up space in most materials prepared for religious schools.

To the performance of mitzvot there is no end. As far as leading a fulfilling Jewish life is concerned, Bar/Bat Mitzvah is only the beginning.

A Personal Note

I am a father. I have a daughter and I love her dearly. I would like my daughter to obey the commandments of the Torah; I would like her to revere me as her father. And so I ask myself over and over again the question: What is there about me that deserves the reverence of my daughter?

You see, unless I live a life worthy of her reverence, I make it almost impossible for her to live a Jewish life. So many young people abandon Judaism because the Jewish models that they see in their parents are not worthy of reverence.

My message to parents is: Every day ask yourselves the question: "What is there about me that deserves the reverence of my child?"

Rabbi Abraham Joshua Heschel
(1907-1972)

By Way of Introduction

Dear Student,

   Your Bar/Bat Mitzvah is one of the most important moments in your life and the life of your family. It is exciting to be able to share the occasion with family, relatives, and friends. It is also one of your first opportunities to become an active leader in congregational prayer. During the service which marks your Bar/Bat Mitzvah, you will lead the congregation in prayers and singing. In assuming this responsibility, you are called *shaliach tzeebor*, literally a messenger for the congregation. You join the prayers of the congregation with your own in order to send them heavenward. Since this is such an important task, it cannot be left in the hands of a child.

   We now call you a Jewish adult. But it is really up to you to become one. When you become Bar/Bat Mitzvah, your rights, privileges, and responsibilities as a Jew change. You are now responsible for your own actions and therefore personally addressed by God's instructions to you in the form of mitzvot. It is also your time to search, study, and accept these new responsibilities as a Jewish adult.

   In various ways, your years of study have helped you prepare for this important point in your life. A long time may pass before you are fully aware of the meaning of these years of preparation. Through this book, we want to help you organize your thoughts and give you an opportunity to learn about mitzvot, then take what you have learned in order to change the world and yourself, one deed at a time.

In this book, you will find an introduction to the concept of mitzvot in Jewish history and tradition. There are twelve units, one for each month of your Bar/Bat Mitzvah year. Each unit focuses on one mitzvah or several related mitzvot. Thus, as you prepare for your Bar or Bat Mitzvah, focus your mitzvah energy—as we like to call it—on the mitzvot described in a particular unit. Each unit contains a little background about the mitzvah, activities, and a project that will allow you to apply each mitzvah in the real world—where it counts. There are also sections of resources for further study intended to enhance and expand your knowledge of Judaism. A journal page is included, as a place to record your personal thoughts and feelings relative to each of the mitzvot.

The choices that you make now will be crucial to the shaping of your life and to making the world a holier place in which to live. The entire Jewish community is depending on you. We hope that you will continue to live a life of "doing mitzvot" beyond your Bar/Bat Mitzvah, living a life of covenant that reflects your relationship with God.

Above all else, may your life be filled with shalom.

Rabbi Ronald H. Isaacs and
Rabbi Kerry M. Olitzky

All About Mitzvot

This section will answer some of the questions you may have about mitzvot. With these explanations in hand, you will be ready to take your first steps on the road to Jewish adulthood and enter into a lifelong dialogue with our tradition. As you learn and do Torah, in the widest sense of the word, you actually become Torah.

What is a mitzvah and how many are there in Judaism?

The word mitzvah (plural: mitzvot) means religious instruction or commandment. Although the word today is often used to mean any "good deed," mitzvah really refers to a specific religious obligation or duty established by the rabbis who lived a long time ago. Generally, we say there are 613 commandments contained in the Torah, although sometimes people disagree on the actual list. There are 248 positive mitzvot ("You should do") and 365 negative ones ("You should not do"). In his book *Sefer Hamitzvot*, written in 1170 C.E., philosopher Moses Maimonides (the RaMBaM) cites the source of each mitzvah in the Torah and teaches us all about it.

What is the connection between a mitzvah and becoming Bar or Bat Mitzvah?

The Bar or Bat Mitzvah is more than just a nice party. Whether you mark the occasion with festivities or not, you now enter the age of responsibility. From now on, you share in the responsibility for Jewish survival. By celebrating your Bar or Bat Mitzvah, you have agreed to be responsible for carrying out the mitzvot. That is what it means to be a Bar (son) or Bat (daughter) of the mitzvot.

In some communities a boy celebrates his Bar Mitzvah when he is thirteen and one day according to his birthdate on the Hebrew calendar and a girl celebrates her Bat Mitzvah at twelve years and one day. In striving to achieve equality among people—something we advocate—many communities celebrate the Bar and Bat Mitzvah at age thirteen for both girls and boys and make the same requirements for both.

What are the various different kinds of mitzvot?

There are different kinds of mitzvot. To make it easier to follow and understand them, we have placed them together in similar groups. Here is a brief summary of some of them:

1. Time-bound and non-time-bound mitzvot

Time-bound mitzvot are those which must be observed at a particular time each day. They should not be observed *whenever* you feel like it. Rather, Jewish tradition establishes a particular time period (with some flexibility) when these mitzvot may be observed. Examples of time-bound commandments include reciting the Shema prayer, putting on tallit and tefillin, and eating matzah during Passover. Since we have rejected the notion that women were not required to observe mitzvot that had to be followed at a particular time because of their responsibilities for raising children and managing household affairs, we invite women to fully participate in the mitzvot. Those mitzvot which are not time-bound, that is, not related to specific times of the day (or year), may be done at any time of day. These include helping the poor, caring for animals, and giving tzedakah.

2. "Light" (less important) mitzvot and "heavy" or "serious" (more important) mitzvot

While mitzvot help us to make our lives sacred, Jewish sages made a distinction between what they called "lighter" and "heavier" mitzvot. For example, Maimonides classified the act of celebrating a festival as a light mitzvah (in Hebrew, *mitzvah kallah*) and the mitzvah of learning Hebrew as a more serious commandment (in Hebrew, *mitzvah chamurah*). This distinction helps us to understand the importance accorded to particular mitzvot in Jewish tradition. As a result, it guides our response to them.

3. Rational and nonrational mitzvot

Not all mitzvot are designed for our minds; many are intended for our souls. The rabbis distinguished between mitzvot for which the reason for doing them was easy to figure out, what we may call "rational," as compared to mitzvot which appeared much less logical, which we may call "nonrational." Most of what we might call ethical mitzvot, such as "do not steal" or "do not kill," are called rational commandments (in Hebrew, *mishpatim*). Keeping kosher is an example of a nonrational mitzvah (in Hebrew *chok* [plural, *chukim*]).

4. Mitzvot which guide our relationships with other people and our relationship with God

The rabbis also distinguished between mitzvot which help us relate to one another (in Hebrew, *mitzvot bayn adam lechavayro*) and those which guide us in our relationship with God (in Hebrew, *mitzvot bayn adam laMakom*). People-to-people mitzvot, as we like to call them, include the prohibitions regarding jealousy of things your neighbor owns and then stealing those things.

Eating in a sukkah, wrapping yourself in a tallit, and putting up a mezuzah on your doorpost are all part of the group of mitzvot which connect you to God because they reflect—in what you do—how you feel about that relationship.

5. Commandments given to Noah's descendants

The rabbis teach us that seven commandments were given to Adam and Noah in Genesis that all people should observe whether they are Jewish or not. Check it out yourself. In Genesis we learn that all people are prohibited from blasphemy, idolatry, incest, bloodshed, robbery, and the eating of flesh from a living animal. In addition, they are required to set up courts of justice.

6. Mitzvot not based in the Torah

There are seven mitzvot which the rabbis determined for us which were not based on any verses in the Torah. Hence, they are called rabbinic mitzvot (in Hebrew, *mitzvot de'rabbanan*). These include: washing one's hands before eating, lighting Shabbat candles, reciting the Hallel psalms, lighting Hanukkah candles, reading the scroll of Esther at Purim, and reciting a blessing when you enjoy something like eating cake. These mitzvot too enhance our lives as Jews.

Special Things About Mitzvot

1. *Simcha Shel Mitzvah,* the joy in doing mitzvot

The rabbis used the phrase *simcha shel mitzvah* to express the joy you feel every time you do a mitzvah. It's a special feeling, one that is very difficult to explain in words. The only way to get the feeling is by doing mitzvot. Mitzvot are not merely part of our obligation as Jews. While some people would like us to believe that mitzvot are burdens, they are what makes being Jewish so special and fill our lives with joy. One sage remarked that the joy of doing a mitzvah was even more pleasing to God than was the mitzvah itself.

2. *Hiddur Mitzvah*, beautifying the mitzvah

Doing mitzvot is not enough. We should also look for ways to make the mitzvah beautiful. That's why we use beautiful *hanukiyot* for lighting Hanukkah candles when any candleholder could be used. That's why we make sure that the mezuzah parchment is enclosed in an attractive mezuzah case when anything that can protect the parchment and keep it attached to the doorpost could actually be used. And that's why we spend so much time decorating the sukkah each year. Essentially *hiddur mitzvah* means doing more than is required to fulfill the mitzvah in a special way.

A person should feed his or her animal before eating.
Babylonian Talmud, Berachot 40a

Mitzvah Project 1

Tzaar Baalei Chayim, Being Kind to Animals

Background

As far back as the Bible, we find several laws which teach us compassion for animals. In the story about Noah and his family in Genesis, one of the so-called Noachide laws (those laws meant to be followed by Jews and non-Jews alike) prohibits the eating of meat taken from a live animal. The mitzvah of observing Shabbat rest (Shabbat M'nucha) is extended to our animals too: ox, donkey, cattle. Wherever we turn, we see that our tradition regards the life of all of God's creatures—animals included—as sacred.

The rabbis also spoke at great length about the responsibility that humans have for animals. At a time in history when animals were apparently treated very cruelly by other peoples, the rabbis taught us the mitzvah of *tzaar baalei chayim,* literally "compassion for the pain of living creatures."

They taught us that people must look after their animals with great care. One of the most insightful instructions in the Talmud concerning the treatment of animals is found in this profoundly simple statement, "You must not eat your own meal until you have seen to it that all your animals have been fed" (Berachot 40a).

Here's what our tradition says:

1. When an ox, sheep, or goat is born, it should stay with its mother for seven days. From the eighth day on, it is acceptable as an offering by fire to God. However, no animal from the herd or flock can be slaughtered on the same day with its young.

Leviticus 22:26-27

2. Do not cook a kid in its mother's milk.

Exodus 23:19, 34:26; Deuteronomy 14:21

3. When you see your enemy's donkey lying under its load and would like to leave it alone, you must nevertheless help it get on its feet.

Exodus 23:5

4. If you come across a bird's nest in a tree or on the ground, and the nest has young birds or even eggs, and the mother is sitting with her young, do not take the mother together with her children. Let the mother go and take only the young—so that you may fare well and live a long life.

Deuteronomy 22:6

5. Do not plow with an ox and donkey together [in the same yoke].

Deuteronomy 22:10

6. If an animal falls into a ditch on the Sabbath, place pillows and bedding under it [since it cannot be moved until the end of the Sabbath].

Babylonian Talmud, Shabbat 128b

7. Rabbi Judah Hanasi (Judah the Prince) observed a calf as it was being led to the slaughterhouse. The animal broke away from the herd and hid itself under Rabbi Judah's clothing, crying for mercy. But Judah pushed it away saying, "Go! This is your destiny!" They said in heaven, "Since he showed no compassion, we will bring suffering to him." For many years after this act, Rabbi Judah suffered a series of painful illnesses. One day, Judah's servant was sweeping the house. She was about to sweep away some young weasels which she found on the floor. "Leave them alone," Judah said to his housekeeper. Subsequently they spoke of Judah [this way] in heaven, "Since he has shown compassion to these rodents, we will be compassionate with him," and he was cured of his illnesses.

Babylonian Talmud, Bava Metzia 85a

8. Compassion should be extended to all creatures, neither destroying nor despising any of them. For God's wisdom is extended to all created things: minerals, plants, animals, and humans. This is the reason the rabbis warned us against despising food. In this way, a person's pity should be extended to all of the works of the Holy Blessed One, just as in God's wisdom, nothing is to be despised. One should not uproot anything which grows, unless it is necessary, nor kill any living thing unless it is necessary. And one should choose a good death for them with a knife that has been carefully examined, to have pity on them as far as it is possible.

Moses Cordovero, *The Palm Tree of Deborah*

9. Jews must avoid plucking feathers from live geese, because it is cruel to do so.

Shulchan Aruch, Even HaEzer 5:14

10. When animals lose their young, they suffer great pain. There is no difference between human pain and the pain of other living creatures.

Moses Maimonides, *Guide for the Perplexed* III:48

HERE'S WHAT YOU DO THIS MONTH:

I. Things to think about

1. Why does the Torah teach us that animals should remain with their parents for a period of eight days before they can be offered as sacrifices?

2. Do you think that people can be motivated to help animals owned by those whom they call their enemies? Why do you think that the Torah includes a law concerning the donkey of one's enemy?

3. Why is it important to allow one's animal to rest on Shabbat? Since we do not use animals very much today for work, how would you define "work" for an animal?

4. Do you believe that eating meat is an act of cruelty toward animals?

5. Based on what you have learned about the mitzvah concerning compassion for animals, what do you think about using animals for medical research?

6. Will this new knowledge about the Jewish approach toward animals change the way you treat your pets and other animals in your community?

7. Do you enjoy visiting the zoo? Based on what you have discovered about Judaism's attitude toward animals, should we keep animals on display in zoos simply for entertainment?

8. What are some things that you can do to help animals in your community? After you have listed them, choose one to do. Make it this month's mitzvah project.

II. According to his writings, the medieval Jewish philosopher Moses Maimonides believed that animals are capable of feeling emotional pain and distress. What do you think? What do scientists believe today about the ability of animals to feel such pain? Do some research and write your findings on the page below.

III. Animals communicate with other animals and people in their own unique ways. How do pets communicate their feelings to you, especially about the way they are being treated? Write your thoughts below.

IV. Vegetarians do not eat meat, because of their concern for the sanctity of the life of animals. Speak to a vegetarian about his or her motivations. Write your notes below and share what you have found out with your class. (If you are a vegetarian, then write your own thoughts below and share them with the class.)

V. According to the Torah, God told Adam and Eve, the world's first humans, that they could only eat food from plants rather than take animals for food. But that's all the Torah tells us. Midrash, the literature which the rabbis used to fill in the details not specified in the Torah, helps us to understand what takes place in the Bible "between the lines." Based on your understanding of the Adam and Eve story, write your own midrash (in the space below) by imagining the conversation that must have taken place between God and the first human beings as they learned that they were prohibited from eating meat. Then read your midrash for other members of your class.

This Month's Mitzvah Project

Make arrangements to visit your local animal shelter. After you have discussed your concerns about the proper treatment of animals with the people responsible for caring for them, develop a program to help. Enlist the help of your friends and members of your family. See which animals in the shelter can be adopted; then try to find people willing to adopt them. Distribute materials in the community about the proper way to care for animals. Make sure that every pet in your neighborhood is licensed and fully inoculated.

My Personal Mitzvah Diary

Tzaar Baalei Chayim, Being Kind to Animals

1. In doing this mitzvah, the most interesting thing I learned was: _____
_____

2. This is how I felt after doing this mitzvah: _____
_____

3. This mitzvah made me more aware of: _____
_____

4. This is how learning about this mitzvah affected me: _____
_____

5. My future goals for this mitzvah are: _____
_____
_____

_____   _____

signature   date

For Further Study

Books

Noah J. Cohen, *Tza'ar Ba'ale Hayim: The Prevention of Cruelty to Animals*. New York: Feldheim Publishers, 1976.

Simon Glustrom, *The Language of Judaism*. New York: Ktav, 1973. See pp. 16-18.

Louis Jacobs, *What Does Judaism Say About . . . ?* Jerusalem: Keter Publishers, 1973. See pp. 24-29.

Judaism and Ecology. New York/Philadelphia: Hadassah and Shomrei Adamah, 1993.

Elijah Judah Schochet, *Animal Life in Jewish Tradition: Attitudes and Relationships*. New York: Ktav, 1984.

Organizations

Canadian Wildlife Federation
(society for the protection of wildlife)
1673 Carling Avenue
Ottawa, Ontario, Canada

Hai Bar Society for the Establishment of Biblical National Wildlife Preserves
(sets up wildlife sanctuaries)
c/o Nature Reserves Authority
78 Yirmeyahu Street
Jerusalem, Israel 94467

Jewish Vegetarian Society
(organization which supports vegetarianism as the appropriate choice for maintaining Jewish dietary laws)
210 Riverside Drive
New York, New York 10025

National Audubon Society
(opposes killing of plumed birds for use of feathers in hats)
700 Broadway
New York, New York 10003

National Wildlife Federation
(emphasizes proper use of natural resources)
1400 Sixteenth Street, NW
Washington, D.C. 20036

World Wildlife Fund
(protects biological resources)
1250 24th Street, NW
Washington, D.C. 20037

To minister to the sick is to minister to God.
Abraham Joshua Heschel

Mitzvah Project 2

Bikkur Cholim,
Visiting the Sick

Background

We all know what it is like to be sick. Unfortunately, some of us know what it is like to be seriously ill. Others among us have even felt the indescribable pain of losing someone we love to a serious illness. While our bodies are amazing examples of God's handiwork, they are not perfect. People in the field of medicine—maybe people you know—are working hard to find more ways to keep us healthy. In the meantime, we still have to confront the reality of sickness and disease. It is the price we pay for being human.

While sometimes very unpleasant, difficult, or even scary, the mitzvah of visiting the sick (*bikkur cholim* in Hebrew) is very important. It is no fun to be sick. And it is horrible to be sick *and* alone. That's one of the many reasons we visit the sick. When we visit those who are ill, through our presence with them, we demonstrate that we care, helping to lift the sick person beyond the burden of illness through our concern and love. The mitzvah of *bikkur cholim*, or visiting the sick, is a mitzvah for people of all ages. Adults should feel a certain sense of obligation and responsibility

for fulfilling this mitzvah. And since you are on your way to becoming an adult, you must join the rest of us in this responsibility.

One of the earliest references in the Bible which concerns *bikkur cholim* is recorded in Genesis (18:1). After Abraham was circumcised, the Torah text tells us that God appeared to him by the terebinths of Mamre. The text then immediately relates to us that Abraham looked up and saw three men standing near the entrance to his tent. Several rabbis suggest that it was God—no messengers or angels for this job—who actually visited Abraham while he was still recuperating to emphasize the importance of the mitzvah of *bikkur cholim*.

Like so many other stories in the Bible, this story about Abraham reflects the human condition. Abraham was sick and God sent messengers to comfort him. In a sense, then, whenever we visit people who are ill—whether we know them or not—we are acting on God's behalf. We, in effect, become God's angels on earth.

Bikkur cholim societies were prevalent in many of the European Jewish communities where our ancestors lived—great-grandparents and beyond. During the last century Jewish immigrants to North America also helped to establish visiting-the-sick societies, which have continued in many communities to this very day. In some congregations and communities, *bikkur cholim* societies have been replaced by caring committees which do essentially the same mitzvah and more. The vocabulary may have changed but the mitzvah work remains the same: caring and comforting those who are ill.

According to the rabbis, there are many things to keep in mind while visiting the sick. Here is a brief summary of the more important things the rabbis want us to remember. Go over the list with a parent, friend, or teacher. Then keep these things in mind when you make your *bikkur cholim* visits. After you have made some visits, you will probably want to add your own insights to the list.

1. Don't stay too long. Lengthy visits may tire the patient.

2. Relatives and friends should visit as soon as the person becomes ill. Distant acquaintances should wait several days before visiting.

3. When visiting, try to enter cheerfully. Be honest and open. Speak from the heart. Do not avoid reality, but do not speak about sad things if at all possible. Leave medicine to the physicians.

4. All people are equal. A so-called important person should visit one who is "less important."

5. Be sensible when visiting someone who is ill, especially if it is difficult for him [or her] to speak. Such visits may be stressful for the patient.

6. When you visit a sick person who is without means, do not visit with empty hands.

Here's what our tradition says:

1. The ancient rabbis regarded visiting the sick as an act of *gemilut chasadim*, a loving act of kindness. As part of their early teachings, the rabbis taught that visiting the sick is one of the mitzvot for which a persons enjoys the fruits in this world, but the real reward is held for the individual in what the rabbis described as the world-to-come.

Babylonian Talmud, Shabbat 127a

2. Rabbi Akiva once visited a disciple who had become ill. No one else had bothered to visit the student. As a result of his illness—and the fact that nobody had come to visit or offer help—the student's house was a mess. Rabbi Akiva rolled up his sleeves and got to work. He even swept the man's floors. When his student recovered, he attributed his restored health to Rabbi

Akiva's visit. Akiva then went out and taught: "One who does not visit the sick is like someone who sheds blood." Rabbi Dimi added: "One who visits the sick causes that person to recover; one who does not visit the sick causes that person to die."

Babylonian Talmud, Nedarim 40a

HERE'S WHAT YOU DO THIS MONTH:

I. Things to Think About

1. When you are sick, how is your state of mind? What kinds of things make you feel better or help you to recover more quickly?

2. What are some of the advantages of people from a particular congregation visiting fellow congregants in the hospital, even those they do not know well?

3. How do you think the vast resources and availability of medical care in modern times affect the mitzvah of visiting the sick?

4. Do you think it is possible to perform the mitzvah of *bikkur cholim* in the same way as our ancestors did?

5. What are some ways that you help someone in your family who gets sick at home?

6. Speak to a parent about the mitzvah of *bikkur cholim?* Do your parents practice it?

II. Invite a rabbi or local hospital chaplain to your class to share his or her experiences with caring for the sick. Record what you have learned below.

III. If there is a local bikkur cholim society in your community, invite a member to discuss its work. If there is not a local visiting-the-sick society, see if you can locate one and research its history. Write your reactions to the presentation in the space below.

IV. Interview a person from a local hospice about experiences related to dealing with patients with life-threatening illnesses. Write the interview questions and responses below.

This Month's Mitzvah Project

Create a small booklet comprised of psalms, prayers, poems, and the like that could be distributed to persons who are ill. Remember to include a selection of the following psalms which can be recited for someone who is ill: Psalms 6, 9, 13, 16, 17, 22, 23, 25, 30, 31, 32, 33, 37, 49, 55, 86, 88, 90, 91, 102, 103, 104, 118, 119, 142, 143. Don't forget to include your own prayers and poetry, as well. As an alternative, create an activity packet of puzzles, stories, projects, and the like. Give them to a friend or relative when they are ill.

Then visit a patient in a local hospital or a resident in a nursing home with your family or with several of your classmates. After sharing your experience with your family, discuss it with your classmates.

My Personal Mitzvah Diary

Bikkur Cholim, Visiting the Sick

1. In doing this mitzvah, the most interesting thing I learned was: _____
_____
_____

2. This is how I felt after doing this mitzvah: _____
_____
_____

3. This mitzvah made me more aware of: _____
_____
_____

4. This is how learning about this mitzvah affected me: _____
_____
_____

5. My future goals for this mitzvah are: _____
_____
_____
_____

_____   _____

signature   date

For Further Study

Books

Philip Birnbaum, *A Book of Jewish Concepts*. New York: Hebrew Publishing Company, 1964. p. 93.

Nina Dubler Katz, *A Training Manual for Bikur Cholim Volunteers*. New York, 1992. (Available by writing to: 130 East 59th Street, Room 306, New York, New York 10022)

Kerry M. Olitzky and Ronald H. Isaacs, *The "How To" Handbook for Jewish Living*. Hoboken: Ktav Publishers, 1993. See pp. 111-112.

Barbara Fortgang Summers, *Community and Responsibility in Jewish Tradition*. New York: United Synagogue Department of Youth Activities, 1978. See pp. 27-42.

Sharon and Michael Strassfeld, *The Third Jewish Catalogue: Creating Community*. Philadelphia: Jewish Publication Society, 1980. See pp. 140-145.

Jane Handler Yurow and Kim Hetherington, *Give Me Your Hand*. Washington, D.C.: 1988.

Organizations

Coordinating Council of Bikkur Cholim
(organization devoted to raising the consciousness of individuals regarding the importance of *bikkur cholim* in the healing process)
130 East 59th Street
New York, New York 10022

National Institute for Jewish Hospice
(the only national Jewish organization which assists individuals who are terminally ill to die with dignity)
8723 Alden Drive
Suite 652
Los Angeles, California 90048

Be happy as you sit at your table
and those who are hungry enjoy your hospitality.
Derech Eretz Zuta 9

Mitzvah Project 3

Hachnasat Orchim, Hospitality

Background

Hachnasat orchim, the notion of extending hospitality to guests and visitors, is an important standard for Jewish behavior. Perhaps because members of the Jewish community know through historical experience what it means to be a traveler, a stranger, this mitzvah developed throughout the centuries as a means of showing personal and community concern for travelers and guests.

One of the most graphic illustrations of this mitzvah focuses on Abraham, Judaism's first patriarch. You can find an example of his hospitality and kindness to strangers in Genesis 18:1-8 (the same text in which we discussed in regard to *bikkur cholim*): "When Abraham raised his eyes, he saw three men standing at a distance from him. As soon as he saw them, he ran from the entrance of the tent door to meet them, and bowed down to the earth and said, 'If I find favor with you, do not pass by your servant. Let a little water be brought so that you may wash your feet, and then rest yourselves under the tree. I will bring you a little food so that you may refresh yourselves.' Abraham ran to the herd, picked out a good, tender bullock, and gave it to his servant who hastened to prepare it." In this selection of text, we see that Abraham hurried to be hospitable to these strangers. Although Abraham had many servants to help him, he himself ran to the herd, because he was eager to personally extend his hospitality to the strangers. It is said that Abraham kept the flaps of his tent open so that he might be able to see people coming from far distances. Then he could run and greet them. It's the Bible's form of "aggressive hospitality."

The ancient rabbis were also very concerned about hospitality. That's why the notion of *hachnasat orchim* occupies a prominent place in sacred literature. For example, the rabbis of Pirke Avot (1:5) teach, "Let your house be open wide, always treating the poor as members of your own family. Rabbi Huna always had the custom of opening the door of his house when he was about to start his meal, and saying, 'Anyone who is hungry may come in and eat'" (Taanit 20b). These same words welcome the visitor to our table at the beginning of our Passover seders. There is also a custom recorded in the Talmud that suggests that people in Jerusalem used to display a flag on their front door. This indicated that the meal was ready and any visitors in the area were welcome to come and eat (Babylonian Talmud, Bava Batra 93b).

The tradition of *hachnasat orchim* was especially apparent among Jewish communities in the Middle Ages. There was even an association dedicated to the task called the chevra hachnasat orchim (society for hospitality to guests). It was kind of like a Traveler's Aid Society that you may have seen in airports, as well as in train and bus stations. These societies even developed a system of meal tickets and youth hostels for scholars and travelers who journeyed from place to place.

Don't wait for a visitor. Invite people to your home, especially for Shabbat and holiday meals when people feel most alone. Let others know that you and your family welcome guests. It is one of the many things that turns a house into a home.

Here's what our tradition says:

As Jewish law began to develop some twenty centuries ago, the rabbis tried to establish specific guidelines for host and guest. Here is a brief summary of these obligations. After reading them, discuss them with your teacher, classmates, and parents. Is this how you treat guests in your home?

Rules for the Host

1. Always be happy when you are sitting at your table and those who are hungry are enjoying your hospitality.

Derech Eretz Zuta 9

2. Do not embarrass your guests by staring at them.

Mishneh Torah, Laws of Blessings 7:6

3. The Jewish court appointed guides to escort those who traveled from place to place.

Mishneh Torah, Laws of the Mourner 14:3

4. It is the obligation of the host to serve at the table. This shows his/her willingness to personally satisfy the guests.

Babylonian Talmud, Kiddushin 32b

Rules for the Guest

1. A good guest says, "How much trouble my host goes through for me!"

Babylonian Talmud, Berachot 58a

2. A good guest complies with every request that the host makes of him [or her].

Derech Eretz Rabbah 6

3. Guests should not overstay their welcome.

Babylonian Talmud, Pesachim 49a

4. Good guests leave food on their plates to show that they have been served more than enough.

Babylonian Talmud, Eruvin 53b

HERE'S WHAT YOU DO THIS MONTH:

I. Things to think about

1. When you attend *tefillah*/worship services at your synagogue, do you ever notice individuals or families whom you have never seen before? Do you approach them during services or at the Oneg Shabbat? What do you think are your responsibilities to guests in the synagogue? What will you do next time you see an individual or family in the synagogue you don't recognize?

2. When guests come to your home, what do you do for them that is special? In what way has the study of this mitzvah changed your behavior with regard to guests in your home?

3. What criteria do you use in order to decide who should receive an invitation to your Bar/Bat Mitzvah? And when they attend, what will you do to host them?

4. Whom should you invite into your home as guests? How about new neighbors and new kids in school for starters?

II. Most communities are made up of people from a variety of places. It is possible that you were not born in the community in which you now live. Are there any families in your community who recently arrived from the former Soviet Union or from other communities outside of the United States? If you don't know their names or addresses, call your local Jewish Family Service or Jewish Federation for help. Then invite a family or two to your home for dinner. Afterwards, write down your thoughts below.

III. Often, synagogues have Shabbat evenings specially devoted to new member families in order to help them get to know others in the community. When your synagogue sponsors such a service, make sure you attend and remember to introduce yourself after services. (You may even decide to invite a new member family to your home for dinner!)

Write a brief summary of the New Member Sabbath held at your local synagogue. What did you most enjoy about the New Member Sabbath?

IV. As an example of how many suburban communities have responded to the challenge of integrating new families into the community, groups called Welcome Wagon have been formed. If such a group has been established in your community, invite one of its member to class in order to discuss the work of Welcome Wagon with members of your class.

If you were to become the head of a Welcome Wagon group, what would be some goals that you would like to accomplish. State them briefly in the space below.

V. HIAS (Hebrew Immigrant Aid Society), as its name suggests, is an organization which was created to assist Jewish refugees and other migrants in their resettlement. It is very likely that HIAS helped settle members of your family when they came to North America. Find out more about this organization, what it has done to help people in your community—and in your family. Perhaps you may want to use some of your Bar/Bat Mitzvah funds to make a tzedakah contribution to the HIAS organization.

Write a brief summary of the HIAS organization and how it operates. Include some of its most recent accomplishments.

VI. *Mazon: A Jewish Response to Hunger is a national organization that donates thousands of dollars each year to assist programs which feed the hungry while teaching us about this important mitzvah. As part of your plans for your Bar/Bat Mitzvah, why not set aside some of the funds which would be spent for your party for Mazon instead. Or ask your guests to contribute the money they would have had to pay for lunch or dinner. For information about the organization and some of the local programs it sponsors, contact Mazon (see address below).*

In the space below, make a list of other things you might do to help Mazon as part of your year of Bar/Bat Mitzvah.

VII. Many communities support a variety of creative activities which provide funds and create public awareness for the hungry. Often, these take the form of walks or runs in which participants solicit sponsors to finance their efforts. One of the more well-known groups which maintain such programs is called CROP. Many synagogues, and other organizations raise thousands of dollars each year by marching in the annual CROP walk, generally held in the fall. It is a great event which often coincides with the celebration of Sukkot. Find out about CROP by writing to the address listed below. If there is CROP walk in your community, make arrangements to participate in it. And try to convince others to join you. In the space below, write an article about your experience (and then send it to the synagogue bulletin or local newspaper). As an alternative, prepare something to be distributed which is designed to persuade people to participate.

VIII. Visit a local food pantry to learn how it collects and distributes food. In the space below, prepare a work plan for you to help the pantry collect food in your school, neighborhood, or community. Perhaps you might want to encourage your family to always buy something extra each time it goes shopping and place this extra item in a food collection box which you have volunteered to maintain in your synagogue.

This Month's Mitzvah Project

Which organizations in your own synagogue perform the important mitzvah of *hachnasat orchim*? Sometimes it is a group of people from the sisterhood or brotherhood (men's club). In the space below, make a list of the kinds of things they do to make people feel at home in your community.

Some communities have interfaith groups sponsored by churches and synagogues which house and feed persons who find themselves without homes. Is your synagogue involved with such a group? Perhaps it sponsors its own food pantry or meals program for the homeless. As an alternative project for this month's mitzvah project, volunteer your time in a local feeding program or housing shelter. Then get your friends and family to help out too. Share the mitzvah!

My Personal Mitzvah Diary

Hachnasat Orchim, Hospitality

1. In doing this mitzvah, the most interesting thing I learned was: _____

_____

_____

2. This is how I felt after doing this mitzvah: _____

_____

_____

3. This mitzvah made me more aware of: _____

_____

_____

4. This is how learning about this mitzvah affected me: _____

_____

_____

5. My future goals for this mitzvah are: _____

_____

_____

_____   _____

signature   date

For Further Study

Books

Philip Birnbaum, *A Book of Jewish Concepts*. New York: Hebrew Publishing Company, 1964. See pp. 110-112.

Simon Glustrom, *Language of Judaism*, Northvale, N.J. Jason Aronson, 1988. See pp. 37-38.

"Hospitality," In *Encyclopaedia Judaica*. Jerusalem: Keter Publishing House, 1972. See vol. 8, cols. 1030-1033.

Tracy Apple Howard with Sage Alexandra Howard. *Kids Ending Hunger: What Can We Do?* New York: Andrews & McMeel, 1993.

Charles Kroloff, *54 Ways You Can Help the Homeless*. West Orange, N.J. and Connecticut: Hugh Lauter Levin Associates and Behrman House, 1993.

_____. *When Elijah Knocks*. West Orange, N.J.: Behrman House, 1992.

Richard Siegel et al., *The Jewish Catalogue*, Philadelphia, Jewish Publication Society, 1973. See pp. 275-276.

Barbara Fortgang Summers, *Community Responsibility in the Jewish Tradition*. New York: United Synagogue Department of Youth Activities. See pp. 9-26.

Organizations

CROP
(organization given to sponsoring walks for the hungry; donors may designate their gifts to any approved hunger-fighting agency)
P.O.B. 968
Elkhart, Indiana 46515

Hebrew Immigrant Aid Society
(philanthropic organization to provide assistance of all kinds to recent immigrants)
200 Park Avenue South
New York, New York 10010

Mazon, a Jewish Response to Hunger
(national organization that raises money to feed the hungry)
2940 Westwood Blvd.
Los Angeles, California 90064

Justice, charity, you shall pursue.
Deuteronomy 16:20

Mitzvah Project 4

Tzedakah, the Righteous Way to Give

Background

The Hebrew word *tzedakah* is often translated as "charity," but that is an imprecise definition. The word "charity" is derived from the Latin word *caritas*, referring to the love of one person for another. The word *tzedakah* comes from the Hebrew word *tzedek*, which means "righteous" or "just." The fact that we use the word *tzedakah* to refer to the righteous way to give teaches us about the Jewish attitude toward charitable giving. Sure, Jews give tzedakah because helping the poor is a loving and kind thing to do. But there's more. Jews do tzedakah because that act helps to eliminate injustice in the world. Thus, tzedakah is the righteous way to give.

Don't expect praise or even thanks when you give tzedakah. After all, we are only doing what we are supposed to do—nothing more. By acting this way, by sharing what we have and by caring for others, we are living the way God intends for us to live. Through tzedakah, we transform thought into deed.

You may be surprised to know that giving tzedakah is required of all people, rich and poor. No matter where we are in life, there are always people less fortunate than we are. All people should know the joy of giving, of fulfilling this important mitzvah.

Here's what our tradition says:

1. When you reap the harvest of your land, do not reap the edges of your field. Also, do not gather the gleanings of your harvest. Do not pick your vineyard bare or gather its fallen fruit. Leave them for the poor and for the stranger. I am Adonai, your God.

Leviticus 19:9-10

2. Open your hand to the poor and your neighbors in your land who are in need.

Deuteronomy 15:11

3. Be generous in giving tzedakah, but beware of giving all that you have.

Babylonian Talmud, Arachin 28a

4. Even a poor person who lives on tzedakah should practice tzedakah.

Babylonian Talmud, Gittin 7a

5. The blessing of tzedakah is greater for the person who gives than the person who receives.

Vayikra Rabbah 34:10

6. The person who gives only a little honestly earned money to tzedakah is better than the person who gives lots of money that has been gained through fraud.

Kohelet Rabbah 4

7. The ultimate purpose of the laws of tzedakah is to nurture in people the quality of mercy and kindness and not just eliminate poverty. God could have accomplished that by providing for the needs of the poor without human intervention.

Sefer Hahinnuch 66, Parashat Mishpatim

8. The highest form of kindness is to help a person to become self-supporting.

Mishneh Torah, Hilchot Matnot Aniyim 10:7-12

9. Tzedakah delivers [the individual] from death.

Proverbs 10:2

10. Hillel used to say: The more tzedakah, the more shalom.

Pirke Avot 2:8

HERE'S WHAT YOU DO THIS MONTH:

I. Things to think about

1. If you were given $500 to use for tzedakah, how would you determine what to do with the money?

2. Complete the following sentence: "When it comes to giving tzedakah, I am very proud that _____

_____

3. What words describe the way you feel when you give tzedakah? To which organizations do you most enjoy giving tzedakah?

4. The rabbis once said that a person who gives tzedakah without anyone knowing about his or her giving is greater than Moses. Do you think that someone who gives tzedakah anonymously is more commendable than one who wants everyone to know about his or her tzedakah gift?

5. The Torah instructs the farmer not to harvest the corners of the field nor collect the produce that might have fallen in the process of harvesting. Thus, the poor must go into the fields and collect the gleanings and harvest the corners of the fields on their own. Would it make more sense for the farmer to harvest the entire field and then give a portion to the poor?

II. The Mishnah describes four kinds of people who give tzedakah: "The person who wants to give but believes that others should not give. The person who wants others to give but will not give himself or herself. The person who gives and wants others to give. And finally the person who will not give and does not want others to give" (Pirke Avot 5:16).

What do you think motivates these kinds of attitudes? Do you know anyone (or have you heard or read about anyone) who fits into these categories? What can you do to change their attitude toward giving? With these things in mind, write your reactions to the Mishnah text in the space below.

III. The Jewish ideals of tzedakah were summarized and taught by Moses Maimonides (called the RaMBaM), a great teacher who lived 800 years ago in Spain and then Egypt. Maimonides believed that tzedakah is like a ladder. It has eight rungs, from bottom to top. Each step you climb brings you closer to Heaven.

1. The person who gives reluctantly and with regret.
2. The person who gives graciously, but less than one should.
3. The person who gives what one should, but only after being asked.
4. The person who gives before being asked.
5. The person who gives without knowing to whom he or she gives, although the recipient knows the identity of the donor.
6. The person who gives without making his or her identity known.
7. The person who gives without knowing to whom he or she gives. The recipient does not know from whom he or she receives.
8. The person who helps another to become self-supporting by a gift or a loan or by finding employment for the recipient.

In the space below, briefly describe a situation you know about which demonstrates each of the eight steps of Maimonides.

This Month's Mitzvah Project

Visit a social service agency, like a nursing home or children's hospital, and arrange to volunteer some time there. While you are there, gather information about it. Find out what you can about the agency. Which organization supports it with funds? Who is helped by its services? And what can you do to help with its mission? Write your plan of action below. Then go out and do it.

My Personal Mitzvah Diary

Tzedakah, the Righteous Way to Give

1. In doing this mitzvah, the most interesting thing I learned was: _____
_____
_____

2. This is how I felt after doing this mitzvah: _____
_____
_____

3. This mitzvah made me more aware of: _____
_____
_____

4. This is how learning about this mitzvah affected me: _____
_____
_____

5. My future goals for this mitzvah are: _____
_____
_____

_____   _____

signature   date

For Further Study

Books

Abraham Eckstein and Azriel Eisenberg, *Tzedakah: A Source Book on Caring and Sharing*. New York: Board of Jewish Education, 1982.

Joel Lurie Grishaver and Beth Huppin, *Tzedakah, Gemilut Chasasdim and Ahavah: A Manual for World Repair*. Denver: Alternatives in Religious Education, 1983.

Jacob Neusner, *Tzedakah: Can Jewish Philanthropy Buy Jewish Survival?* New York: Rossel Books, 1982.

Lillian Ross, *Not Charity But Justice*. Miami: Central Agency for Jewish Education.

Danny Siegel, *Tell Me a Mitzvah*. Rockville, Md.: Kar-Ben, 1993.

Organizations

American Jewish Joint Distribution Committee
(aids Jews in need of health, welfare, cultural, and religious services)
60 East 42nd Street
New York, New York 10017

United Jewish Appeal
(major national organization through which American Jewish communities channel support for humanitarian programs of social welfare in Israel and in Jewish communities throughout the world)
1290 Avenue of the Americas
New York, New York 10019

Ziv Tzedakah Fund
(organization dedicated to Danny Siegel's unusual approach to giving)
263 Congressional Lane #708
Rockville, Maryland 20852

Honor your father and your mother.
Exodus 20:12

Mitzvah Project 5

Kibud Av Va'eym, Honoring Parents

Background

The mitzvah of honoring parents is taken directly from the fifth of the *aseret hadibrot*. We generally call these mitzvot the Ten Commandments, but they are really more like "ten statements" from Sinai. The first five statements reflect the relationship between a person and God. The last five are addressed to the relationship between people. The fifth commandment, *kibud av va'eym*, honoring parents, has often been called the link between the two groups of mitzvot, because when one honors one's parents, one is also honoring God.

The mitzvah of *kibud av va'eym* is one of the few mitzvot in the Torah with a promise attached to it, what we call part of the covenantal relationship (from the word "covenant," *brit*) we have with God. Placing it in the Torah this way stresses its importance: "Honor your mother and father, so that your days may be long on the land that God gives you." According to the Mishnah, honoring parents is one of the mitzvot for which one is rewarded in this world *and* the world-to-come (Peah 1:1).

In order to help us understand what "honoring one's parents" means in everyday life, the rabbis teach us that *kibud av va'eym* includes, for example, providing them with food, drink, and clothing, as well as guiding their footsteps when they grow old. These are really adult responsibilities. That's what being Bar/Bat Mitzvah is all about. Such things are not left for children to do.

As if that were not enough, in the Book of Leviticus we are also taught that we are to "revere" our parents: "A person should revere his [or her] mother and father" (Leviticus 19:3). As would be expected, the rabbis debated what it means to revere one's parents. Some said that it means to literally stand in awe of them. Others suggested that it means that we should respect them because we are afraid of them. According to one interpretation, to revere one's parents means that we should not sit in their chair, speak in their place, or contradict what they say (Sifra to Leviticus 19:3). In other words, nothing like, "No—you're wrong!" in response to things they say. It may take some practice not to say these words, but we know you can do it!

Here's what our tradition says:

1. When persons honor father and mother, God says, "I credit such action as if they had honored me."

Babylonian Talmud, Kiddushin 30b

2. When Rabbi Dimi came, he said, "Dama son of Nethinah was once wearing a gold-embroidered silk cloak, sitting among Roman nobles. When his mother came, she tore it off of him, hit him on the head, and spat in his face. Yet, he did not shame her."

Babylonian Talmud, Kiddushin 31a

3. If you see your parents transgressing a mitzvah, do not say to them, "Father, Mother you have disregarded a precept from the Torah." Rather, you should say, "Such-and-such is written in the Torah," speaking to your mother and father as though you were consulting then instead of admonishing them.

Mishneh Torah, Mamrim 6:11

4. Honor your father and your mother just as you honor God, for all three have been partners in your creation.

Zohar III, 93a

5. Shimon bar Yochai said, "To honor one's parents is even more important than honoring God."

Jerusalem Talmud, Peah 15d

6. Rabbi Judah Hanasi taught, "It is revealed and therefore known to God that a son honors his mother more than his father because she influences him through words. Therefore, with regard to the mitzvah of honoring parents, the father precedes the mother."

Babylonian Talmud, Kiddushin 30b-31a

7. One should not call one's parents by their first name, either during or after their lifetime, except to identify them to others.

Based on *Mishneh Torah*, Mamrim 6

I. Things to think about

1. How do you honor your father, your mother? Have you ever discussed this idea with either parent?

2. How do you define honor?

3. Do you receive any kind of reward for honoring your parents?

4. Do you honor one parent more than the other? Are you afraid of either parent?

5. Why do you think that the Torah includes the promise of long life for those who honor their parents?

6. In our North American culture, we observe Mother's Day and Father's Day. Do you believe that you give your parents more honor on these days? If so, in what way?

7. If you choose to become a parent and are blessed with children, how would you want them to show honor to you?

8. Why do you think that there is no specific mitzvah that instructs you to love your parents?

II. In the space below, describe an ideal parent. Which things in your list match your mother or father? Have you ever discussed these things with either parent? Well, now's the time to do so.

III. There are lots of parents and children in the Bible. Some of the kinds of things they do may be similar to things that happen in our own families. Of the things you have read about in the Bible, when do the biblical parents seem to deserve the respect of their children? In the space below, describe what took place that warrants such respect.

IV. In the Book of Proverbs (3:9), it is written, "Honor God with substance. Just as you must honor God even if there is financial loss, you must honor your parents even if you lose money as a result of it."

This is really an adult mitzvah. Think about it. What could you do for God—or your parents—as part of your desire to honor them that might cause you to lose money? Once you have figured out something, write it down in the space below.

V. We have already learned that Rabbi Judah Hanasi taught, "It is revealed by God that a male fears his father more than his mother, for it his father who teaches him Torah. Thus, with regard to the mitzvah of fearing one's parents, the mother is placed before the father." Today, we may question this tradition, but we are still obligated to try to understand it. It's part of the challenge of inheriting a tradition.

In a few paragraphs below, consider how to respond to these questions: Why did Rabbi Judah Hanasi relate the teaching of Torah to fear? Which parent is more involved in your Jewish education? Why?

VI. Has there ever been a time when your parents asked you to do something but you didn't want to since you had plans to do something with your friends? It's often hard to balance your own desires with the obligation you also have to fulfill the mitzvah of honoring your parents. What advice would you give someone who comes to you for help with this mitzvah, who may have scheduling conflicts of his or her own? Write what you might say in the space below.

VII. We have learned what honor and respect for parents means as far as the rabbis are concerned. What do you think that the rabbis meant when they said:

Their interpretation   Your interpretation

Don't sit in your parent's place.

Don't contradict your parent's words.

Give your parents food and drink.

Help your parents in and out.

This Month's Mitzvah Project

Family tensions often run high in preparation for major league events like Bar/Bar Mitzvah. There are lots of preparations, arrangements for out-of-town relatives, and plenty of studying to do. During this month, keep a journal which reflects your interactions with your parents. After each interaction, try to record what took place and whether you indeed fulfilled the mitzvah of honoring parents. Discuss it with your parents. Then determine what all of you can do to help you try to better live up to the expectation of the mitzvah.

My Personal Mitzvah Diary

Kibud Av Va'eym: Honoring Parents

1. In doing this mitzvah, the most interesting thing I learned was: _____
_____
_____

2. This is how I felt after doing this mitzvah: _____
_____
_____

3. This mitzvah made me more aware of: _____
_____
_____

4. This is how learning about this mitzvah affected me: _____
_____
_____

5. My future goals for this mitzvah are: _____
_____
_____

_____   _____
signature   date

61

For Further Study

Books

David M. Feldman, *The Jewish Family Relationship*. New York: United Synagogue, 1975. See pp. 17-26.

Simon Glustrom, *The Language of Judaism*. Northvale, N.J.: Jason Aronson, 1988. See pp. 161-162.

Louis Jacobs, *The Book of Jewish Practice*. West Orange, N.J.: Behrman House, 1987. See pp. 54-59.

Joel S. Wasser, *We Are Family*. New York: United Synagogue of America, 1991.

Study is greater than practice because it leads to practice.
Babylonian Talmud, Kiddushin 40b

Mitzvah Project 6

Talmud Torah, the Study of Torah

Background

Because the Torah is the touchstone of the Jewish people, we are often called the "people of the book." The book, of course, is the Torah. But Torah is more than just one book. It refers to all of Jewish sacred literature and learning. The rabbis emphasized the study of Torah because the study of Torah leads a person to the observance of other mitzvot.

We find the instruction to study Torah wherever we turn in Jewish tradition. Torah study was not encouraged only to sharpen one's mind, but also to serve as a guide for living a moral life. The logic goes this way: One who takes Torah study seriously will most likely choose the right path in life. For this reason, the mitzvah of Torah study outweighs all of the other commandments. The rabbis of the Talmud wrote: "These are the things for which a person enjoys the dividends in this world while the principal remains for the person [to enjoy] in the world-to-come. They are: honoring parents, loving deeds of kindness, making peace between one person and another, but the study of the Torah is equal to them all" (Shabbat 127a).

In the first paragraph of the Shema, which is derived from the Book of Deuteronomy, we are charged to express our love for God through constant study: "when you lie down and when you rise up." Such study has the potential to bring us into a closer relationship with God. Torah study sweetens one's life. To emphasize this sweetness, children, especially in Eastern Europe, used to begin their study of Hebrew with letters that had been written in honey. As they learned their letters and enjoyed the honey, they also learned that the study of Torah was sweet.

In a sense, Bar/Bat Mitzvah is like the first day you began your Jewish studies as a child. As an adult, you begin again—with a commitment to lifelong study of Torah. Now the decisions you make are your own. And you are responsible for the results of those decisions. Thus, what you get out of such study will depend solely on what you put into it. It can be boring and tedious if you approach the text that way. Or you can soar heavenward if you are willing to do it.

Consider how you approach the text. The goal of the study of Torah extends beyond the reading of the text. By studying about our biblical ancestors, we enter their lives. Their struggles become our struggles, their challenges our challenges. We become them and they become us. And at the end of this process, they leave a little bit of themselves in us and we leave a bit of ourselves in them—until we are prepared to enter into this dialogue once again.

Here's what our tradition says:

1. The world stands on three things: on Torah, worship, and loving deeds of kindness.

Pirke Avot 1:2

2. Judah ben Tema was fond of saying, "At five [one begins the study of] the Bible. At ten the Mishnah. At thirteen [one takes on] the [responsibility for] the mitzvot. At fifteen [one begins the study of] the Talmud.

Pirke Avot 5:21

3. Make your home a regular meeting place for scholars.

Pirke Avot 1:4

4. Be a disciple of Aaron: love peace and pursue it; love your neighbors and attract them to Torah.

Pirke Avot 1:12

5. Shammai taught: Make the study of Torah your primary pursuit.

Pirke Avot 1:15

6. Do not say "When I have some free time, [then] I'll study." You may never have that leisure.

Pirke Avot 2:5

7. One who has acquired Torah has acquired eternal life.

Pirke Avot 2:8

8. If you have studied much Torah, your reward will be abundant.

Pirke Avot 2:21

9. Without sustenance, there can be no Torah. And if there is no Torah, there can be no sustenance.

Pirke Avot 3:21

10. The Torah is a tree of life for those who cling to it. All who uphold it are happy.

Proverbs 3:18

HERE'S WHAT YOU DO THIS MONTH:

I. Things to think about

1. How can the Torah hold up the world? In what way do you think that Torah study is one of the pillars which supports the world?

2. How is the Torah a tree of life to those who cling to it? What about those who do not study Torah?

3. Based on what you have already studied, what do you think are three of the most important verses in the Torah? Why do you consider them so important?

4. While we may speak about the world-to-come, none of us is sure what that really means. After all, we will have to wait until messianic time to figure it out. Yet, our tradition suggests that Torah study can provide us with life in the world-to-come. Regardless of what you may specifically think about the world-to-come, how can Torah study provide us with entrée into that world?

5. The rabbis teach us that the reward for the study of Torah study is abundant. What do you think the rabbis meant by this statement? Perhaps the reward comes from the study of Torah itself. What do you think?

II. As would be expected, Jewish tradition has a great deal to say about the study of Torah. Do some library research and find a text—one line is enough—that best expresses how you feel about Torah study. Write it down and explain it in your own words in the space below. Then illustrate it.

III. Choose a book with a Jewish subject. After you have read it and spent some time thinking about its message, share what you have learned with your family. Then write a one-page summary below emphasizing the main points. Remember to include whether or not you would you recommend this book to others. Don't forget to include the reasons for your recommendation.

IV. If your community is lucky enough to have a Jewish museum or gallery, why not visit it with your family. Perhaps you may want to choose another place of Jewish interest. Describe your visit in the space below, including the things you learned when visiting it.

V. Prior to beginning study, one recites the following blessing: Baruch ata Adonai, Elohenu Melech Haolam, asher kidshanu b'mitzvotav v'tzivanu la'asok b'divrei Torah, "Praised are You, Adonai our God, Guide of all the Universe, who made us special through mitzvot and instructed us to study Torah." Using your own words, translate the blessing in the space below. Think about why it is necessary to offer a blessing prior to the study of Torah.

Now take a look at the Kaddish Derabbanan, the Rabbis' Kaddish, a special prayer which concludes study and is said in memory of all of the teachers and students who came us and studied Torah. As we study Torah, we are a link in the chain of tradition of Jews who study Torah.

VI. Find out which colleges and universities in your area offer courses in Jewish studies. List the courses that each institution has to offer. Next to each course, try to explain how that course may be considered part of the study of Torah in its widest sense. Place an asterisk next to the courses that most appeal to you.

VII. Listed below are four teachers whose work significantly impacted on the way Judaism is studied and observed up to this day. Spend some time in your school library in order to learn a little about these great teachers. Then, next to each name, identify the important contribution each made in the history of Jewish study.

a. Rabbi Akiva:

b. Rashi:

c. RaMBaM:

d. Rabbi Joseph Caro:

This Month's Mitzvah Project:

This month, get into the habit of studying the weekly Torah portion. Read it over several times during the week. Saturday afternoon is a perfect time for intensive study. Choose a traditional commentator as well as modern one to help guide you. Discuss it with a parent. Consider the life of the individuals in the narrative material. What message does their life have to offer your own?

My Personal Mitzvah Diary

Talmud Torah, the Study of Torah

1. In doing this mitzvah, the most interesting thing I learned was: _____ _____ _____

2. This is how I felt after doing this mitzvah: _____ _____ _____

3. This mitzvah made me more aware of: _____ _____ _____

4. This is how learning about this mitzvah affected me: _____ _____ _____

5. My future goals for this mitzvah are: _____ _____ _____

_____   _____

signature   date

For Further Study

Joel Grishaver, *Being Torah*. Los Angeles: Torah Aura Productions, 1985.

___, *Learning Torah*. New York: Union of American Hebrew Congregations, 1990.

Leonard Kravitz and Kerry Olitzky, *Pirke Avot: A Modern Commentary on Jewish Ethics*. New York: Union of American Hebrew Congregations, 1993.

Louis Jacobs, *The Book of Jewish Practice*. West Orange, N.J.: Behrman House, 1987.

Lawrence Kushner and Kerry Olitzky, *Sparks Beneath the Surface: A Spiritual Commentary on the Torah*. Northvale, N.J.: Jason Aronson, 1993.

Sharon and Michael Strassfeld, *The Second Jewish Catalogue*. Philadelphia: Jewish Publication Society, 1976.

When you wage war against a city,
. . . do not destroy its trees.
Deuteronomy 20:19

Mitzvah Project 7

Bal Tashchit, Don't Destroy

Background

The rabbis tell us a story in the Midrash (Ecclesiastes Rabbah to 7:13) that, following the creation of humankind, God took Adam and Eve around the Garden of Eden. God showed them all of its beauty, then said to them: "See how beautiful is my handiwork. I have created all of it for you to use. Please take care it. Do not spoil or destroy my world." This story really reflects the text taken from Deuteronomy which is quoted at the beginning of this chapter: "When you wage war against a city, and you have to besiege it in order to capture it, do not destroy its trees, wielding an ax against them. You may eat from them, but you must not cut them down."

This is where the mitzvah of *bal tashchit* is derived. From this verse, which forbids the cutting down of fruit-bearing trees, the rabbis of the Talmud extended the principle prohibiting willful destruction of any object from which someone might benefit.

The rabbis of the Talmud could never have imagined that human beings would someday ravage the earth as extensively as we are witnessing today. The Industrial Revolution gave us so much, but it came at the cost of cutting down trees, destroying farmland, polluting the air, and dumping toxic waste into our rivers and streams. It is our responsibility to do all that we can do to protect the earth and the environment.

Perhaps one of the most amazing things about the relationship between nature and human beings can be found in the midst of Shabbat. We were given six days to manage the earth, often interfering with the natural order of things. But on Shabbat, we are instructed neither to create nor destroy. Instead, on Shabbat we simply enjoy the beauty of the universe and acknowledge God as Creator of it all.

Just as the Sabbath provides us with a balance for the work week, Jewish agricultural laws related to what is called the "sabbatical year" provide for the needs of the land. The Bible (Exodus 23:11) declares that a Jewish farmer is permitted to sow and reap for six years, but the seventh year is set aside as a sabbath so that the earth may be renewed.

The message of our tradition is clear and precise for Bar/Bat Mitzvah students and for all who populate this planet earth. The earth belongs to God. As God's people, we are merely the caretakers of the earth. Therefore, we must do all that we can to take care of it. It is the only one we are going to get!

Here's what our tradition says:

1. Care is to be taken that bits of broken glass should not be scattered on public land where they may cause injury. Pious people often buried their broken glassware in their own fields.

Babylonian Talmud, Baba Kamma 30a

2. A tannery must not be set up in such a way that the prevailing winds can send the unpleasant odor to the town.

Jerusalem Talmud, Baba Batra 2:9

3. While it is the practice to cut one's garment on hearing of the death of a close relative [often called "cutting *keriah*"], tearing too much or too many garments violates this principle.

Babylonian Talmud, Baba Kamma 91b

4. Whoever breaks vessels, tears clothes, demolishes a building, stops up a fountain, or wastes food, in a destructive way, transgresses the law of *bal tashchit*.

Mishneh Torah, Melachim 6:10

5. It is forbidden to destroy animals.

Babylonian Talmud, Chullin 7b

6. It is forbidden to cause the oil in a lamp to burn too quickly, thus wasting fuel.

Babylonian Talmud, Shabbat 67b

HERE'S WHAT YOU DO THIS MONTH:

I. Things to think about

1. What are some things that you have been given for which you feel responsible? How do you take care of these things?

2. Deuteronomy 20 asks: "Are trees of the field human?" In what ways are trees similar to human beings?

3. There are several rabbis who equate the destruction of things with idolatry? What do you think is the connection between idolatry and destruction?

4. What are some of the ways that we waste natural resources in our own homes, schools, and synagogues?

5. In Deuteronomy 11, we read God's promise to reward us with rain and sufficient food if we follow the mitzvot. What does this promise have to do with caring for the environment?

6. Some environmentalists say that all of our actions have environmental consequences? Do you agree?

II. *The mitzvah of bal tashchit teaches us the importance of not being wasteful. Write down some of the ideas which you might suggest to others that might help them not to waste things.*

III. Convince a group of your fellow students to help you pick up litter on the grounds of your synagogue or school. In the space below, describe how you are going to convince them. Once you have accomplished your task, write a brief report about your experience.

IV. This is a tough one. What is more important: saving a forest of 1,000 acres or cutting the trees for a housing development which would provide jobs for lumberjacks and builders? Divide the space below into two columns, one for the advantages and one for the disadvantages. Then make your list. Which list is longer or more important?

V. Since we live in controlled environments, we are often very isolated from the cycles of nature. In what ways can the agricultural aspects of the three festivals—Sukkot, Pesach, and Shavuot—help to remind us that we should bring our lives into better harmony with nature? Write your thoughts below.

VI. Using pictures and not words, draw a picture which reflects your own understanding bal tashchit.

VII. With your teacher's permission, of course, ask each of your classmates to bring in one item of trash. Then brainstorm ways each of these items might be reused or recycled. Design a recycling guide in the space below. Then copy it for students in other classes.

This Month's Mitzvah Project

Develop a recycling campaign for your neighborhood. Help your neighbors to devise effective ways of separating out recyclable materials. If you do not have curbside pickup for recycling, develop a strategy for collecting materials in your neighborhood. Remember, if you are all driving to the recycling station for the same things, then you are wasting energy too. After you have finished your project, go plant a tree. No matter how much recycling we do, there is always unintentional destruction of God's creations.

My Personal Mitzvah Diary
Bal Tashchit, Don't Destroy

1. In doing this mitzvah, the most interesting thing I learned was: _____
_____
_____

2. This is how I felt after doing this mitzvah: _____
_____
_____

3. This mitzvah made me more aware of: _____
_____
_____

4. This is how learning about this mitzvah affected me: _____
_____
_____

5. My future goals for this mitzvah are: _____
_____
_____

_____   _____

signature   date

For Further Study

Books

Ellen Bernstein and Dan Fink, *Let the Earth Teach You Torah*. Wyncote, Pa.: Shomrei Adamah, 1992.

Simon Glustrom, *The Language of Judaism*. Northvale, N.J.: Jason Aronson, 1988.

John Javna, *50 Simple Things Kids Can Do to Save the Earth*. Kansas City: Andrews & McMeel, 1990.

Ya'akov Kirschen, *Trees, the Green Testament*. New York: Vital Media Enterprises, 1993.

Lillian Ross, *The Judaic Roots of Ecology*. Miami: Central Agency for Jewish Education, 1986.

Jeffrey Schrier, *Judaism and Ecology*. Washington, D.C.: Hadassah and Wyncote, Pa.: Shomrei Adamah, 1993.

Organizations

Air Pollution Control Association
(group that wants to clean up the air by controlling the amount of pollution we put in it)
4400 Fifth Avenue
Pittsburgh, Pennsylvania 15213

The Conservation Foundation
(dedicated to the conservation of natural resources)
1250 Connecticut Avenue
Washington, D.C. 20036

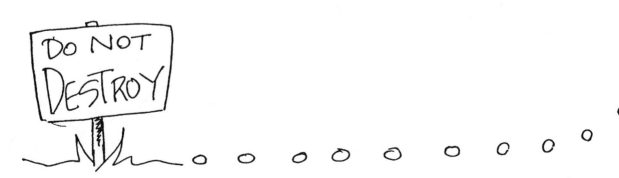

Department of the Interior
Water Pollution
(government agency which enforces the government policy which allows/disallows the placement of industrial waste in water)
Washington, D.C. 20202

Friends of the Earth
(organization committed to protecting the earth and its resources)
30 East 42nd Street
New York, New York 10017

Shomrei Adamah
(Jewish organization committed to the preservation of the earth)
Church Road and Greenwood Avenue
Wyncote, Pennsylvania 19095

Weeping may linger at night, but joy comes with the dawn.
Psalm 30:6

Mitzvah Project 8

Chesed Shel Emet, Honoring the Dead and Comforting Mourners

Background

Chesed shel emet means a "true act of kindness" and is used to refer to caring for the dead since no one can accuse the individual of doing the mitzvah for personal gain. After all, the person who is being served by the mitzvah is dead. As a result, this act of kindness—and everything that goes along with it—is highly praised in Jewish tradition.

Often people don't want to discuss death. Some are uncomfortable thinking about preparing a human body for burial. Such discussions may remind us of our own mortality, the reality that we too will die one day. Nevertheless, the preparation and burial of the human body, along with comforting the mourners for the person who has died, has traditionally held a place near the top of the ladder of doing mitzvot.

One of the earliest references to burial is found in the Book of Deuteronomy. There we read that "a person must not let a human body remain on the stake overnight, but must bury it the same day" (Deut. 21:23). From this verse, the rabbis deduced that it is preferable to bury a dead person within twenty-four hours, unless there are circumstances which prevent it. Things that might delay burial include waiting for out-of-town relatives to attend the funeral.

Thus, we have the obligation to care for the dead and comfort the living.

Here's what our tradition says:

There are a whole array of customs, traditions, and legal requirements related to caring for the human body following death. While most of the ones listed below are in the category of halacha (Jewish law), and are not regarded as binding by liberal Jews, many may be considered customs and traditions. Here is a brief summary of some of the most significant ones:

1. *Shemirah* (watching the body): From the moment of death until burial, according to traditional Jewish law, the deceased may not be left alone. Many communities arrange for a *shomer* ("watchperson") to be at the side of the deceased at all times. This person, or several persons taking turns, will often recite psalms and meditate throughout the "watch."

2. *Tahara* (ritual purification): This act is usually performed by members of the chevra kaddisha (burial society). This volunteer organization is charged with watching the body of the deceased and dressing it in white linen shrouds (symbolizing purity), a simple garment made of white linen or cotton. In the past, cemeteries had their own rooms to perform the ritual of purification. Today, the washing of the body usually takes place on the premises of the funeral home.

3. It is traditional to allow the body to decompose naturally. Therefore, embalming (injecting the deceased with chemicals to prevent decay) and cremation are frowned upon by Jewish law. However, some liberal Jews have chosen to embalm or cremate for a variety of reasons.

4. Casket: The general principle which governs Jewish rituals at death is equality. Thus, whether a person was rich or poor, they become equal at death—as they were equal when they entered this world. As a result, most traditional Jews understand that traditional burial should take place using a simple wooden coffin. Friends of the deceased are often asked to carry the coffin to the grave at the cemetery as pallbearers. This act is another example of true kindness, which is selfless and can never be repaid.

5. Burial: At the gravesite, mourners and friends often cover the coffin with spadefuls of dirt. On hearing the clods of earth fall against the casket, the mourners begin to realize that the person whom they loved is really dead. However difficult, it is an important step toward accepting the reality of death.

6. *Shiva*: Following the burial, or interment, as it is often called, the mourner usually returns to the home of the deceased to sit *shiva*. Taken from the Hebrew word for "seven," *shiva* refers to the first seven days of mourning. During this period, the family of the deceased stays together. This gives them the mutual support and comfort necessary to face the challenge of death. During *shiva*, friends and community members, as well as other members of the family, visit to express their sympathy and sadness. In order for the individuals who are mourning to focus on their loss, but also because friends are concerned that the mourners eat properly, the first meal following the funeral, called the meal of condolence, is provided by friends. This is another way that friends extends themselves to mourners. Most times, there is nothing that can actually be said to soften the pain. Just being there and reaching out to people can help them with the pain they feel. Making

a *shiva* call, visiting a *shiva* house (you will hear both expressions), is not a social event. Avoid small talk. Remember that the mitzvah is to visit the mourners and help comfort them. Prayer services (often referred to simply as a minyan) will generally take place at the home of the mourners during *shiva* so that they will be able to recite the Mourner's Kaddish without leaving their home.

At the end of *shiva*, the mourner literally walks around the block to signify the end of the first period of mourning. After the period of *shiva*, the mourner slowly reenters routine life. The first month, called *sheloshim* (for "thirty" days), reflects the first step back to routine living. During this period and the months that follow for the year (*shana*), as difficult as it may be, we try to comfort the mourner.

HERE'S WHAT YOU DO THIS MONTH:

I. Things to think about

1. Why do you think that the rabbis regarded preparing a human body for burial as a sincere act of kindness?

2. Why does Jewish tradition discourage cremation?

3. How did the custom develop that friends and family of the deceased place shovelfuls of earth into the grave? What purpose does it serve?

4. Do you think that people who have just experienced the death of someone they love are in a position to make their own decisions about funeral arrangements and the like? What should the community do to help them?

5. In general, what can the synagogue community do to help mourners during *shiva* and afterwards after the individual moves into the periods of less intense mourning called *sheloshim* and *shana*?

6. Why is participation in a chevra kaddisha (burial society) considered so important?

II. The pain of losing someone we love can be all-consuming, robbing the individual of the ability to think clearly for a period of time. Some people believe that a burial society, since it is voluntary and nonprofit, prevents unscrupulous individuals from taking advantage of mourners during this time of intense pain. In the space below, list some abuses that might occur in communities in which a burial society does not function.

III. According to Jewish tradition, we are supposed to proclaim: "Praised be the righteous Judge" when we learn of the death of a loved one. In a short paragraph, explain why you think that the rabbis chose these words to be said at such a time.

IV. Find out what things are done in your community for mourners during shiva. Put a check mark next to those that you—or members of your family—have done for people.

V. If your community has a chevra kaddisha, contact one of its members and interview him or her about the activities of the burial society. Before you meet with that person, write down your questions below.

VI. In many communities, there are Jewish funeral homes. In other communities, non-Jewish funeral homes are taught what needs to be done to accommodate Jewish burial customs. Interview the local funeral director responsible for Jewish funerals. Find out what services are provided for families that have lost a loved one. Make a list of those services below.

VII. There are a variety of opinions about life after death, especially within the various movements in the Jewish community. Do you believe in life after death? Do some research on the Jewish views of life after death, then write down your thoughts below.

VIII. In the Talmud, Rabbi Yochanan teaches us that "Comforters are not permitted to say a word until the mourner begins the conversation" (Babylonian Talmud, Moed Katan 28b). What do you think motivated Rabbi Yochanan to make that suggestion? Do you agree with his advice? What kind of advice would you give people when they are going to visit a mourner in order to try to comfort him or her? Write your own guidelines on this page.

This Month's Mitzvah Project

While some gravesites have what is called "perpetual care" and others have caretakers responsible for the grounds, many cemeteries, especially older ones, are poorly maintained. Through your synagogue, find out which Jewish cemeteries in your community need to be cleaned, leaves raked, bushes pruned, headstones turned upright. For this month's project, spend some time with your classmates sprucing up the cemetery. You will learn a great deal about your community and those who came before you at the same time.

My Personal Mitzvah Diary

Chesed Shel Emet,

Honoring the Dead and Comforting Mourners

1. In doing this mitzvah, the most interesting thing I learned was: _____

_____

_____

2. This is how I felt after doing this mitzvah: _____

_____

_____

3. This mitzvah made me more aware of: _____

_____

_____

4. This is how learning about this mitzvah affected me: _____

_____

_____

5. My future goals for this mitzvah are: _____

_____

_____

_____   _____

signature   date

For Further Study

Books

Arnold M.Goodman, *A Plain Pine Box*. Hoboken, N.J.: Ktav, 1981.

Ronald H. Isaacs and Kerry M. Olitzky, *A Jewish Mourner's Handbook*. Hoboken, N.J.: Ktav, 1991.

Ronald H. Isaacs et al., *Chain of Life: A Curricular Guide about Death, Bereavement and the Jewish Way of Honoring the Dead*. New York: Coalition for Advancement in Jewish Education, 1993.

Maurice Lamm, *The Jewish Way in Death and Mourning*. New York: Jonathan David, 1969.

Audrey Marcus et al., *Death, Burial and Mourning*. Denver: Alternatives in Religious Education, 1976.

Jack Riemer, *Jewish Reflections on Death*. New York: Schocken Books, 1976.

Rifat Sonsino and Daniel Syme, *What Happens After I Die?* New York: UAHC Press, 1990.

Organizations

Bereaved Parents
(nationwide organization intended to guide and comfort parents who have suffered the loss of a child)
1717 South Puget Sound
Tacoma, Washington 98405

Compassionate Friends
(nationwide organization intended to guide and comfort parents who have suffered the loss of a child)
P.O.B. 3696
Oak Brook, Illinois 60521

Compassionate Friends of Canada
Les Amis Compatissants du Canada
685 William Avenue
Winnipeg, Manitoba R3EOZ2

Fernside: A Center for Grieving Children
(program designed to help children who have experienced loss, especially the death of a parent)
P.O.B. 8944
Cincinnati, Ohio 45208

Jewish Funeral Directors of America
(professional organization that provides a great deal of information for the general public)
399 East 72nd Street, Suite 3F
New York, New York 10021

Commitments are an aid to self-control.
Pirke Avot 3:17

Mitzvah Project 9

Nedarim, Keeping Commitments

Background

Judaism is a religion of concepts and values which are deeply invested in words. The power of words when spoken in the form of an oath or promise is linked to a belief in God, in whose name that vow is made. You've undoubtedly heard expressions like "In the name of God" and "I swear to God." While we may not take these expressions as seriously as we should, and often consider them merely figures of speech, the Bible and Jewish tradition take such statements very seriously. Listen to the advice of Proverbs: "Death and life are in the power of the tongue" (Proverbs 18:21).

Whether we call it a vow or a promise or simply one's word, one must keep a commitment. It is tied to one's belief in God and in God's presence in the world and in our lives. The Torah teaches us that a person who makes a vow, a promise to God, or takes an oath to do something, must carry out that promise (Numbers 30:3).

The third of the ten Sinai statements, the Ten Commandments, states that we should not utter the name of God in vain. Take a look at Exodus 20:27. There we learn that one should not make a promise casually, without considering the consequences. The ancient rabbis were not at all enthusiastic about people taking oaths. They understood the power of promises. In the Talmud, the rabbis wrote that "it is better to make no promises at all than to make them even if one is certain of fulfilling them" (Chullin 2a).

The most well-known statement about promises and vows comes to us on the evening of Yom Kippur in the form of the Kol Nidre. This unusual declaration specifies that all the promises we have made to God that have gone unfulfilled are null and void. Kol Nidre was probably originally designed to protect Jews who had been forced to convert to Christianity in order to save their lives. It allowed them to make Christian promises without being fearful that they had turned their backs on Jewish tradition.

The latest of the comprehensive Jewish law codes, the *Shulchan Aruch*, which was compiled by Rabbi Joseph Caro in the sixteenth century, devotes a great deal of space to the laws of promises and vows. While the details are quite specific, this is an example of how seriously the Jewish community has considered vows over the last few centuries. The following warning, borrowed from the Talmud, opens the chapter on vows in this Code of Jewish Law: "Don't get into the habit of making vows. The one who makes a vow is called wicked."

We can even see remnants of this fascination with vows and promises in modern Hebrew. The popular Hebrew expression *blee neder* (literally, "without a vow"), when said with regard to something that the speaker promises to do, is in keeping with the idea that we are expected to do everything that we say we are going to do.

Here's what our tradition says:

1. Vows are a fence for abstinence.

Pirke Avot 3:13

2. The making of vows is the doorway to folly.

Kallah Rabbati 5

3. A person who utters a vow places a burden or his [or her] neck.

Jerusalem Talmud, Nedarim 9:1

4. Be careful what you vow, and don't get into the habit of making vows, for if you get in the habit, you will, in the end, sin by breaking your oath, and anyone who breaks his or her oath denies God without hope of pardon.

Tanchuma, Mattot 79a

NEDARIM

I. Things to think about

1. Did you ever make a promise that you knew you could not keep? What prompted you to do so? Are there any times that we can make promises about things that we have no intention of keeping?

2. Did you ever make a promise that you wanted to keep but were unable to do so? How did you feel? What did you do to remedy the situation?

3. What do you think should happen to people who do not keep their promises?

II. *Read the Kol Nidre prayer. Then write a modern-day Kol Nidre in the space below.*

KOL NIDRE

ALL VOWS, PLEDGES, OATHS, PROMISES WE MAKE TO YOU, BETWEEN THIS YOM KIPP BE NULL AND VOID

III. Using the library, find out what you can about the Nazirites, a special group of people described in the Bible who made several special vows to God. What were these vows? What do you think about the Nazirites? Could you emulate their way of life?

IV. Why do you think that Jewish tradition discouraged people from making vows and promises? Using what you know about Jewish history, write your answer in the space below.

V. Why are promises often so difficult to keep? Identify several promises that God made to the Israelites in the Bible? Did God fulfill the promises? Describe what happened below.

This Month's Mitzvah Project

Over the next four weeks, keep a diary of all of the vows, promises, and commitments you make—even when you say "I'll do it" to a parent when asked to do something. Take note of how many of them you were able to keep, as well as what you plan to do with regard to the obligations that were not fulfilled. Then go do what you promised to do.

My Personal Mitzvah Diary
Nedarim, Keeping Commitments

1. In doing this mitzvah, the most interesting thing I learned was: _____

_____

_____

2. This is how I felt after doing this mitzvah: _____

_____

_____

3. This mitzvah made me more aware of: _____

_____

_____

4. This is how learning about this mitzvah affected me: _____

_____

_____

5. My future goals for this mitzvah are: _____

_____

_____

_____   _____

signature   date

For Further Study

Books

Philip Birnbaum, *A Book of Jewish Concepts*. New York: Hebrew Publishing Co., 1964.

_____, ed., *Maimonides' Mishneh Torah*. New York: Hebrew Publishing Co., 1967. See book VI, section on vows.

Bernard Novick, *Making Jewish Decisions About the Body*. New York: United Synagogue Department of Youth Activities, 1980.

Stephen Rittner, *Jewish Ethics for the 21st Century*. Boston: Stephen Rittner, 1977. See chap. 10: "Ethics of Communication."

The prosperity of a country
is in accordance with the treatment of its aged.
Rabbi Nachman of Bratzlav

Mitzvah Project 10

Hiddur P'nai Zaken, Esteeming the Elderly

Background

As a result of improved health care and nutrition, and better living conditions all around, there are more older adults alive today then at any other time in history. While the life-spans of many personages in the Bible were of disproportionate length, what we read as "years" may mean periods of only six months, and thus the lives described in the text may not have been as long as we imagine. And in other cases, the ages of biblical characters are used as metaphors to reflect extremely long-lived ancestors. Even so, Jewish tradition has always been sensitive to the needs of the elderly. While most people would like us to believe that sacred literature simply advocates for the elderly, it is not true. While older adults are generally held in high esteem by our tradition, the historical perspective on growing older is far better balanced. There is a recognition of both the wisdom accrued through life experience and the physical challenge of growing older.

Listen to the words of Leviticus (19:32): "Rise before the aged and show respect to the elderly." This passage instructs us to treat older adults with respect. A link between the characteristic needs of the aged and acts of kindness and consideration is found in many works of Jewish literature. Throughout Jewish history, the elders were sought for advice because they had participated in so many of life's experiences. We read in Pirke Avot (4:28) this verse: "A person who learns from the young may be compared to one who eats unripe grapes and drinks wine from a vat, but a person who learns from the old may be compared to one who eats ripe grapes and drinks wine that is aged." Nonetheless, in the personal poetry of the Book of Psalms (71:9-10), we hear the plaintive cry of the older adult: "Do not reject us in our old age; do not abandon us when our strength has left us. Even in old age with gray hair, do not abandon me until I have declared Your strength to the next generation, Your might to everyone that has yet to come." Nevertheless, Psalm 92, the psalm intended to be read each Sabbath day, concludes with the famous line: "Even in old age righteous people will continue to bear fruit; they will be full of vigor and strength."

When the aged needed support to live independently and the family lacked the necessary resources, the Jewish community provided assistance. Yet, it was not until modern times that this group of elderly—what we sometimes call the vulnerable elderly—was treated as a separate group,

113

apart from the sick and the poor in the community. Thus, societies for the aged and homes for the aged developed in North America in the nineteenth century. The first Jewish home for the aged in the United States was established in St. Louis in 1855. During the next century, most cities with large Jewish communities established Jewish homes for the elderly. We must remember, however, that only 5 percent of the older adult population at any one time resides in nursing homes and similar facilities. Most older adults are the heads of their own households, living in their own houses and apartments.

Today, many—but not enough—synagogues and Jewish community centers have specialized programs for older adults. Much more than basket weaving and bingo, these programs provide services for the elderly while also providing them with opportunities to study and continue to grow as human beings and as members of the Jewish community with a great deal to contribute.

HERE'S WHAT YOU DO THIS MONTH:

I. Things to think about

1. The Bible teaches us that "love your neighbor as yourself" is one of the most important of all the mitzvot in the Torah. It is probably one of the most difficult, as well. How do you go about fulfilling it when "your neighbor" is elderly?

2. In the Passover Haggadah, we are reminded that when Rabbi Elazar ben Azariah was seventeen years old he said the following: "Look, I feel like a person who is seventy years old." What

motivated him to say this? What do you think he had in mind? Do his words reflect a positive or negative attitude toward growing older?

3. What are some ways in which you can help the elderly?

4. How do you feel that the elderly are characterized in movies and on television? Do you think that such stereotyping reflects reality?

5. The Book of Job (12:12) states that "with the aged comes wisdom, and length of days brings understanding." Do you agree with this statement? What experiences have you had to support or undermine Job's claim.

II. The Bratzlaver Rebbe, Rabbi Nachman, once said that "the prosperity of a country is in accordance with the treatment of its aged." Do you agree with what Rabbi Nachman said? Do you feel that the elderly are treated appropriately in the United States and Canada? What about Israel? Write your answers below.

III. List below the names of some elderly people whom you know well. Briefly describe them. Do they have needs that are different from your own, or are they like you, only much older? Which of their needs can be met in formal services provided by the Jewish community? Which of their needs can't be satisfied at all? Write your answers below on this page.

IV. Visit a local nursing home, home for the aged, retirement community, or any other "aged-segregated facility" as they are called. Share your experiences with your classmates and log your visit below.

V. Many synagogues have an annual Sabbath service for grandparents and great-grandparents. If your synagogue has one, describe the service and how older adults are uniquely involved in it.

VI. Here's a research project for you. It will take you to the library. With the help of a parent or teacher, make a list of several persons who have made significant achievements at age sixty-five or older. (This seems to be the magical number for entrance into older adulthood in our society.) Find out a few details about these individuals and write what you learn on the page below. Do you think that their age impacted on their contribution to society?

VII. Write your reactions to the following statement in Pirke Avot (4:25): "Elisha ben Abuya said, 'When a person learns [something] while still a youth, it is similar to ink written on new paper. When a person learns [something] as an older person, it is like writing with ink on paper that has already been erased.'"

VIII. Interview a physician who specializes in working with older adults—called a geriatrician—and ask him or her what kinds of physical changes can be expected as people grow older, especially regarding the five senses. Given these physical changes, what kinds of things need a synagogue do in order to provide a supportive environment for older adult members? Write down your ideas in the space below.

This Month's Mitzvah Project

    With the help of your parents and teachers, identify an older adult living in his or her own home in your community whom you can help to maintain independent living and personal dignity. Your goal is to help to create a supportive environment in order for this to happen.

    As an alternative, select an older adult with whom you want to study something, a text, a skill, even the weekly Torah portion. Invite that person to be your religious mentor so that you may benefit from his or her experience of living. In this way, the older adult can truly become living Torah for you.

HIDDUR PNAI ZAKEN

My Personal Mitzvah Diary
Hiddur P'nai Zaken, Esteeming the Elderly

1. In doing this mitzvah, the most interesting thing I learned was: _____
_____
_____

2. This is how I felt after doing this mitzvah: _____
_____
_____

3. This mitzvah made me more aware of: _____
_____
_____

4. This is how learning about this mitzvah affected me: _____
_____
_____

5. My future goals for this mitzvah are: _____
_____
_____

_____   _____
signature   date

For Further Study

Books

Abraham Chill, *The Mitzvot: The Commandments and Their Rationale*. Jerusalem: Keter, 1974. See chapter on respect for the elderly.

Dorothy C. Herman, *From Generation to Generation*. Miami: Central Agency for Jewish Education, 1985.

Kerry M. Olitzky, ed., *"The Safe Deposit" and Other Stories About Grandparents, Old Lovers and Crazy Old Men*. New York: Markus Weiner, 1989.

Kerry Olitzky and Lee Olitzky, *Aging and Judaism*. Denver: Alternatives in Religious Education, 1980.

Barbara Fortgang Summers, *Community Responsibility in Jewish Tradition*. New York: United Synagogue of America, Department of Youth Activities, 1978.

Magazines

"Growing Older." *Keeping Posted*, vol. 27, no. 6, April 1982.

Organizations

Consult your local Jewish Federation, Jewish Family Service, or Jewish Community Center for information regarding their work with the elderly. In some larger communities, there are organizations sponsored and supported by the Jewish community which focus only on the elderly in the community.

Dorot

(organization providing services only for New York area elderly, but its programs are models which can be duplicated throughout the country)

171 West 85th Street

New York, New York 10025

What is hateful to yourself, do not do to your neighbor.
Babylonian Talmud, Shabbat 31a

Mitzvah Project 11

V'ahavta L'reyacha, Loving One's Neighbor

Background

According to Rabbi Akiva, "loving your neighbor as yourself" (Leviticus 19:18) is the most important mitzvah in the entire Torah. Two thousand years ago, when a non-Jew challenged Hillel to teach him the whole Torah while he stood on one foot, Hillel answered: "What is hateful to you, do not do to your neighbor. That is the entire Torah—all the rest is commentary. Go and learn it" (Babylonian Talmud, Shabbat 31a).

It all sounds great and pretty easy. But it is not so easy. Do we love a neighbor with the same love we have for a parent or a friend or even ourselves? Love is difficult to describe and place in concrete terms. It does not seem like something that can be willed. Thus, how can anyone be instructed or commanded to love? And how can we love neighbors, many of whom we may not even know? Thus, we must learn to behave toward others (whether, in fact, we like them or not) as we would want them to behave toward us. The verse asks us to act properly. Actions can be commanded.

The mitzvah of loving one's neighbor as oneself has been expanded in the codes of Jewish law to include the importance of visiting the sick, comforting the mourner, and even making a bride and groom happy. Concern for one's neighbor includes a concern for his/her moral and spiritual growth. The Torah (Leviticus 19:17), therefore, asks us not to simply rebuke a neighbor who is doing wrong but to keep rebuking until the neighbor mends his/her ways. If we do want to warn anyone, we must do so in a kind and gentle manner, always pointing out that we have only one goal in mind: to reach out and extend a helping hand to a friend.

Perhaps it has been our ability to reach out to a fellow Jew in need that has helped our people to survive. All Israelites—all Jews—are linked together as brothers and sisters, say the sages.

In modern times, the philosopher Martin Buber built his philosophy called "I-Thou" around the mitzvah of loving one's neighbor, teaching that we should never treat other people as things or objects, but as human beings like ourselves!

Here's what our tradition says:

1. Hatred stirs up strife, but love draws a veil over all transgressions.

Proverbs 10:12

2. The person who truly loves another can read the other's thoughts.

The Koretzer Rebbe

3. What is hateful to you, do not do to your neighbor. This is the whole of Torah. All the rest is commentary.

Babylonian Talmud, Shabbat 31a

4. Whoever destroys a single life, it is as if that person had destroyed the entire world.

Mishnah Sanhedrin 37

5. When love is strong, we can lie on the edge of a sword.

Mishnah Sanhedrin 72

I. Things to think about

1. Think about your neighbors, those who live next door or in the neighborhood. Do you feel that you have fulfilled the mitzvah of loving them as much as you love yourself? Can you do more?

2. Some people believe that a true leader is one who can turn an enemy into a friend. Do you feel that this is even possible? Have you ever met someone whom you thought you wouldn't like and you ended up as friends?

3. Does the mitzvah of loving your neighbor as yourself truly mean that you must like everyone?

4. If you have two neighbors and they both need your help, how do you decide which neighbor to help first?

II. What are some ways that people show that they care about their neighbors? List some examples below.

III. Which organizations in your community are based on the fundamental principle of loving your neighbor? List the organizations and briefly describe how they serve your neighborhood or community.

IV. In order to teach this mitzvah to younger children, write a short story describing how a person can turn an enemy into a friend.

FROM FOE TO FRIEND . . . .

A STORY 4 LITTLE KIDS BY

V. In order to teach us an ethical principle, the rabbis of the Babylonian Talmud (Baba Metzia 62a) describe the case of two persons who are lost in the desert. One of them has a water bottle. The is not enough water for two, so if they share it, both will surely die. If only one of them drinks the water, he or she may survive. What should these people do? If you were in a similar situation, what would you do? Create a storyboard in the space below to describe your answer.

This Month's Mitzvah Project

This month, participate in a community service project to help your neighbors. Then write a brief report of your experiences on this page.

My Personal Diary

V'ahavta L'reyacha, Loving One's Neighbor

1. In doing this mitzvah, the most interesting thing I learned was: _____
_____
_____

2. This is how I felt after doing this mitzvah: _____
_____
_____

3. This mitzvah made me more aware of: _____
_____
_____

4. This is how learning about this mitzvah affected me: _____
_____
_____

5. My future goals for this mitzvah are: _____
_____
_____

_____   _____
signature   date

For Further Study

Books

Louis Jacobs, *The Book of Jewish Belief*. New York: Behrman House, 1984.

Moses Maimonides, *The Commandments*. New York: Soncino Press, 1967. See vol. 1, pp. 220-221.

Barbara Fortgang Summers, *Community Responsibility in the Jewish Tradition*. New York: United Synagogue Department of Youth Activities, 1978.

Organizations

The Abraham Fund

(supports programs which promote understanding between Arabs and Jews in Israel)

477 Madison Avenue

New York, New York 10022

Interns for Peace

(designed to promote understanding between Arabs and Jews in Israel)

165 East 56th Street

New York, New York 10022

Remember the Sabbath day and keep it holy.
Exodus 20:8

Mitzvah Project 12

Shemirat Shabbat, Observing Shabbat

Background

Since ancient times, Shabbat has been singled out as the most important celebration in Judaism. We sometimes forget this, but Shabbat is more important than Rosh Hashanah and Yom Kippur. Think about it: Shabbat is the only holiday included in the Ten Commandments. The fourth commandment states explicitly: "Remember the Sabbath day to keep it holy. Work for six days, but on the seventh day, which is a sabbath of God, do not do any work."

In responding to the mitzvah to stop working on Shabbat and transform it into a day of rest and renewal, we are following God's pattern of creative labor. God created the heavens and the earth and all the living creatures, and then God rested. We, in imitation of God, rest as well! But Shabbat also teaches us that while we should live our lives in reflection of our covenant with God, we are mortal and must cease work.

To make sure that we stop work and enhance the holiness of the Sabbath day, the ancient rabbis defined what they meant by work, and specified various categories of labor that were not permitted on Shabbat. The Mishnah (Shabbat 7:2) lists thirty-nine categories of work that are prohibited by traditional Jewish law. They include plowing, planting, tying and untying knots, cutting, writing, building, demolishing, lighting a fire, and extinguishing a fire. These activities reflect the day-to-day life of the ancient Jewish community. Throughout history rabbis have used them as a basis for guiding our activities on Shabbat. For example, some people do not use electricity on Shabbat since it is like making fires. For many modern liberal Jews, however, we are interested in the spirit of Shabbat as well as its particular laws and prohibitions. Whatever you decide about Shabbat, we all agree that nothing on Shabbat is as important as saving a human life. Therefore, even in the most traditionally observant community, Shabbat laws are suspended whenever human life is at risk.

Shabbat is not all prohibitions. It is an opportunity to get a taste of the messianic, a glimpse of how the world can be. We prepare to celebrate Shabbat and then enjoy the experience of Shabbat with prayer, festive meals, singing, resting, relaxing, and yes some study too. Shabbat is a time to rest mind and body, to appreciate the many things in our world that we often do not take enough time to notice during the work week. It is also a time to be with family and friends, an occasion to reflect on the past week and gather the strength to begin a new one.

Shabbat, therefore, reflects the spiritual side of being human. It is one of the reasons that we measure time in relation to Shabbat. For whatever are our labors during the week, we look forward to each Shabbat with eager anticipation and the luxury it affords us to be refreshed and renewed for the week ahead. Remember: however you choose to observe the Sabbath, make it special.

And don't forget to make Havdalah when you are finished.

Here's what our tradition says:

Ahad Ha'am, a famous Jewish philosopher, once summarized the importance of the Sabbath to the people Israel with this well-known statement: "More than Israel has kept the Sabbath, the Sabbath has kept Israel."

I. Things to think about

1. Why do you think that Shabbat was the only holiday to be mentioned in the Ten Commandments?

2. Why are candles lit as part of the way we welcome Shabbat into our homes?

3. Why were wine, spice, and fire chosen to be used in Havdalah ceremony? What do these three objects symbolize?

4. What do you find on your family's Shabbat table?

5. We make *motzi* over bread because it symbolizes all the food we eat. On Shabbat, we use two challot as we recite the blessing over bread at the Shabbat meal. Why do we need two loaves of bread?

6. What are some things that you can do with your family to prepare for Shabbat?

II. Write a poem about the importance of Shabbat. Try to include your own experience of Shabbat in your poem.

III. The instruction to observe Shabbat appears twice in the Torah. In the Book of Exodus, we are told to "remember" the Sabbath. However, in the Book of Deuteronomy we are told to "observe" the Sabbath. In the space below, try to explain the difference between these instructions. For help, reread the verses in Exodus (20:17) and Deuteronomy (5:1-18). As you are writing, consider whether the observance of Shabbat impacts on Jewish survival.

IV. How is it that Shabbat can give us a taste of the world-to-come? What is it all about? After you have had a chance to discuss this with some folks, perhaps even your rabbi, write down what you think about the rabbinic description of the world-to-come as one continuous Shabbat.

V. Many years ago, the rabbis decided that criminals could not be punished on Shabbat. Why do you think the rabbis made this decision? What does it tell you about how the rabbis felt about Shabbat? How can we adapt this concept to the criminal justice systems in the United States and Canada?

VI. During the year, a variety of special Sabbaths occur. These reflect the journey of the Jewish people in Torah, as well as the holiday cycle. How are these special Sabbaths observed in your congregation? Write a few sentences about each one in the space below.

This Month's Mitzvah Project

Write down four things that you would like to do in order to make Shabbat more meaningful for yourself and for your family. Then over the next four weeks, introduce these things—one each week—into your Shabbat observance. A helpful hint: you may want to discuss them with your parents ahead of time.

SHEMIRAT SHABBAT

My Personal Mitzvah Diary

Shemirat Shabbat, Observing Shabbat

1. In doing this mitzvah, the most interesting thing I learned was: _____

_____

_____

2. This is how I felt after doing this mitzvah: _____

_____

_____

3. This mitzvah made me more aware of: _____

_____

_____

4. This is how learning about this mitzvah affected me: _____

_____

_____

5. My future goals for this mitzvah are: _____

_____

_____

_____   _____

signature   date

For Further Study

Books

Malka Drucker, *Shabbat: A Peaceful Island*. New York: Holiday House, 1983.

Stephen Garfinkel, *Slow Down and Live: A Guide to Shabbat Observance and Enjoyment*. New York: United Synagogue Department of Youth Activities, 1982.

Michael Strassfeld, *A Shabbat Haggadah*. New York: Institute of Human Relations Press, American Jewish Committee, 1981.

Ron Wolfson, *Shabbat: The Art of Jewish Living*. New York: Federation of Jewish Men's Clubs, 1985.

ADDITIONAL MITZVAH OPPORTUNITIES
_____

1. Israel Bonds Young Builders Program. Contact your local Israel Bonds office or its national office at 575 Lexington Avenue, New York, New York 10022.

2. Intergenerational Bar/Bat Mitzvah (parent-child B'nai Mitzvah).

3. Make a presentation to the synagogue in honor of your Bar/Bat Mitzvah.

4. Prepare a letter to the congregation to be included in your invitation or shared during your ceremony reflecting on the question, "What my Bar/Bat Mitzvah means to me."

5. Plant trees in Israel in honor of your Bar/Bat Mitzvah. Contact the local office of the Jewish National Fund or its national office at 42 East 69th Street, New York, New York 10021.

6. Prepare an oral history of your family. Then send it as a historical record to the American Jewish Archives, 3101 Clifton Avenue, Cincinnati, Ohio 45220.

7. Use your Bar/Bat Mitzvah to seek publicity for a social action campaign to whose cause you are committed. Remember to include it in your Bar/Bat Mitzvah speech.

8. Save for a trip to Israel through the Gift of Israel Bar/Bat Mitzvah registry or the Gift of Israel Savings Plan. For information, contact your local Jewish Federation or the Council of Jewish Federations at 730 Broadway, New York, New York 10003.

9. Participate in the "Bar/Bat Mitzvah Matching Program" sponsored by the World Union of Progressive Judaism (838 Fifth Avenue, New York, New York 10021). For a gift of $100, the World

Union for Progressive Judaism will match your Bar/Bat Mitzvah with a Russian Jewish student. Funds will be used to supply religious schools in Russia with needed educational materials.

10. After you have budgeted for your Bar/Bat Mitzvah, send 3 percent to MAZON: A Jewish Response to Hunger. Invite your guests to do the same. Contact MAZON at 2940 Westwood Boulevard, Los Angeles, California 90064.

Changing: As a Jewish Individual in Society. State of Israel Ministry of Education and Culture, 1984.

Benjamin Efron and Alvan D. Rubin, *Coming of Age: Your Bar/Bat Mitzvah.* New York: Union of American Hebrew Congregations, 1979.

> A basic introduction to the historical Bat/Bat Mitzvah and its relevance for young Jewish people today.

Azriel Eisenberg, *The Bar Mitzvah Treasury.* New York: Behrman House, 1952.

> A classic collection filled with rich resources from the Jewish tradition about the Bar/Bat Mitzvah.

Shoshana Glatzer et al., *Coming of Age as a Jew: Bar/Bat Mitzvah.* New York: Board of Jewish Education, 1989.

> While designed as a curricular supplement, this is really a very nice textbook for Bar/Bat Mitzvah students.

Audrey Friedman Marcus et al., *A Family Unit on Bar and Bat Mitzvah.* Denver: Alternatives in Religious Education, 1977.

> An excellent unit for B'nai/B'not Mitzvah families for study and celebration; accompanied by an excellent resource guide prepared by Rabbi Kerry M. Olitzky.

Bert Metter, *Bar Mitzvah, Bat Mitzvah: How Jewish Boys and Girls Come of Age*. New York: Clarion Books, 1984.

> A gentle introduction to Bar/Bat Mitzvah written for the student who has had little experience in Jewish life-cycle contexts and few expectations for the Bar/Bat Mitzvah.

Jacob Neusner, *Mitzvah*. Chappaqua, N.Y.: Rossel Books, 1982.

> An excellent introduction to the world of mitzvot for young people in user-friendly language.

Moira Paterson, *The Bar Mitzvah Book*. New York: Praeger, 1975.

> Gives background and advice, all you need to know to plan a meaningful Bar/Bat Mitzvah.

Stephen Rittner, *All That You Want to Know About Bar-Bat Mitzvah*. Boston: Stephen Rittner, 1976

> A creative introduction to Bat/Bat Mitzvah by a creative Bar/Bat Mitzvah teacher. You will certainly enjoy using this book as your prepare for your studies.

Jeffrey Salkin, *Putting God on the Guest List*. Woodstock, Vt.: Jewish Lights Publishing, 1993.

> Designed to help us as families restore meaning to what is the most significant event in our growing years.

There are a variety of companies which have basic software for computer-assisted Bar/Bat Mitzvah training. As technology gets more sophisticated and easily accessible for home use, more products will undoubtedly become available. For further information, contact Davka Corporation at 7074 N. Western Avenue, Chicago, Illinois 60645 or Lev Software at P.O. Box 17832, Plantation, Florida 33318.

You may also be interested in the Torah La-Am Library, which is interactive, features a Hebrew/English translation of the Torah, and has over 10,000 items of midrash, stories, and commentary on CD-ROM. Contact Torah Productions, 3070 North 51st Street, Suite 510A, Milwaukee, Wisconsin 53210.

Your Bar/Bat Mitzvah: Parashah and Haftarah booklets are available (with a liberal Jewish commentary) UAHC Press, 838 Fifth Avenue, New York, New York 10021. In addition, audiocassettes of chanted selections of these portions (with blessings) are available from Transcontinental Music, 838 Fifth Avenue, New York, New York 10021.

Hanafter Bar Mitzvah pamphlets available at Shilo Publishing Company, 73 Canal Street, New York, New York, 10002.

Other helpful publications:

The Bar Mitzvah Book. New York: Praeger Publishers, 1975.
Harvey Fields, *A Torah Commentary for Our Times* (3 vols.). New York: UAHC Press, 1991-93.
Carol Kur, "Invitation to a Bar Mitzvah: Rites and Wrongs of Passage," *Moment Magazine,* December 1981, pp. 37-41.
Seymour Rossel, *The Bar Mitzvah and Bat Mitzvah Handbook: A Spiritual Journey.* West Orange, N.J.: Behrman House, 1993.
Michael and Sharon Strassfeld, *The First Jewish Catalogue.* Philadelphia: Jewish Publication Society, 1976. See pp. 61-81.